FOOD LOVERS

LUNCH

RECIPES SELECTED BY JONNIE LÉGER

Trans
Atlantic
Press

All recipes serve four people, unless otherwise indicated.

For best results when cooking the recipes in this book, buy fresh ingredients and follow the instructions carefully. Make sure that everything is properly cooked through before serving, particularly any meat and shellfish, and note that as a general rule vulnerable groups such as the very young, elderly people, pregnant women, convalescents and anyone suffering from an illness should avoid dishes that contain raw or lightly cooked eggs.

For all recipes, quantities are given in standard U.S. cups and imperial measures, followed by the metric equivalent. Follow one set or the other, but not a mixture of both because conversions may not be exact. Standard spoon and cup measurements are level and are based on the following:

1 tsp. = 5 ml, 1 tbsp. = 15 ml, 1 cup = 250 ml / 8 fl oz.

Note that Australian standard tablespoons are 20 ml, so Australian readers should use 3 tsp. in place of 1 tbsp. when measuring small quantities.

The electric oven temperatures in this book are given for conventional ovens with top and bottom heat. When using a fan oven, the temperature should be decreased by about 20–40°F / 10–20°C – check the oven manufacturer's instruction book for further guidance. The cooking times given should be used as an approximate guideline only.

CONTENTS

SPICY SWEET POTATO SOUP with GINGER — 4

PEPPERS with SPINACH and MONKFISH STUFFING — 6

ASPARAGUS RISOTTO — 8

POTATO SALAD with SMOKED TROUT — 10

STUFFED TOMATOES — 12

SPAGHETTI with SHRIMP and COCONUT SAUCE — 14

RICE SALAD with LENTILS — 16

MINI SAVORY TARTS — 18

BEAN and CHEESE QUESADILLAS — 20

EGG NOODLES with CHICKEN and VEGETABLES — 22

PENNE with TOMATOES and GORGONZOLA — 24

SPINACH and EGG STRUDEL — 26

CREAMY CORN CHOWDER — 28

EGG AND TOMATO WRAP — 30

LENTIL SOUP with HAM — 32

CHICKEN SALAD PITAS — 34

HUMMUS and SPROUT PITAS — 36

MISO SOUP with VEGETABLES — 38

SALMON in PUFF PASTRY with YOGURT DIP — 40

CHICKEN and MANGO SALAD — 42

ASPARAGUS and POTATOES with CREAMY HOLLANDAISE SAUCE — 44

FRITTATA with SMOKED SALMON and MASCARPONE — 46

SPICY SWEET POTATO SOUP WITH GINGER

Ingredients

2 tbsp. olive oil

2 orange colored sweet potatoes, peeled and cubed

2 onions, finely chopped

1 clove garlic, finely chopped

½ inch / 1 cm piece fresh ginger, finely chopped

2 tbsp. sherry vinegar

4 cups / 1 liter vegetable broth (stock)

½ cup / 100 ml whipping cream

Salt & pepper

1 pinch cinnamon

¾ cup / 75 g goat cheese

Shredded scallion (spring onion), to garnish

Method

Prep and cook time: 30 min

1 Heat the oil in a saucepan and sauté the prepared ingredients. Now pour in the vinegar and the vegetable broth (stock), cover with a lid and simmer for about 15 minutes until the sweet potatoes are soft.

2 Purée the soup with a hand blender and mix in the cream and a little liquid (broth or milk) until the soup has the desired consistancy. Bring to a boil again and season with salt, pepper, and cinnamon.

3 Ladle the soup into bowls, crumble some goat cheese over the top, garnish with scallions (spring onions) and serve.

PEPPERS WITH SPINACH AND MONKFISH STUFFING

Ingredients

4 red bell peppers

2 tbsp olive oil

2 shallots, finely chopped

2 cloves garlic, minced

About 3 cups /100 g spinach leaves

1 bunch basil, leaves separated and chopped (reserve a few leaves for garnish)

½ bunch parsley, chopped

½ lb / 250 g monkfish, cut into bite-size chunks

Salt and freshly ground pepper, to taste

½ cup / 100 ml vegetable broth (stock), divided

Method

Prep and cook time: 50 min

1 Preheat the oven to 350°F (180°C / Gas Mark 4).

2 Blanch the bell peppers: slice off the top third of each to make a lid and remove the cores. Fill a large bowl with ice water. Bring a large saucepan of salted water to a boil. Add the peppers and their lids; cook for 8-10 minutes; quickly remove them with a slotted spoon to the ice water to cool. Drain.

3 Heat the oil in a skillet; add the shallots and garlic and sauté until translucent. Add the spinach, basil and parsley and cook until the spinach wilts. Then mix in the monkfish, season with salt and pepper and remove from the heat. Drain in a sieve and squeeze lightly. Stuff the bell peppers with the fish and spinach mixture, put on the lids and stand upright in a baking dish. Add the vegetable broth (stock) and bake for about 15 minutes, until cooked through.

4 Put the stuffed bell peppers on warmed plates. Serve with rice and garnish with basil.

ASPARAGUS RISOTTO

Ingredients

1 lb / 500 g asparagus, trimmed

1 pinch sugar

Salt, to taste

2 tbsp butter, divided

1 shallot, finely diced

2 cups / 400 g risotto rice

1 cup / 250 ml dry white wine

2 cups / 500 ml vegetable broth (stock)

2/3 cup / 60 g freshly grated Parmesan cheese, plus additional for sprinkling

Method

Prep and cook time: 50 min

1 Cut off the tips from the asparagus and reserve. Thinly slice the stalks.

2 To cook the asparagus tips, bring ½ cup / 200 ml water, the sugar and a pinch of the salt to a boil in a saucepan. Drop in the asparagus tips and cook for about 5 minutes, until al dente. Remove from the pan, reserving the cooking liquid, and transfer to a colander under cold running water to stop the cooking; set aside.

3 Heat 1 tablespoon of the butter in a deep skillet until it foams, then add the asparagus slices and shallot and sauté until tender. Add the rice, stir well and sauté briefly.

4 Mix the wine with the reserved asparagus water and vegetable broth (stock). Pour 2 ladlefuls of the mixture onto the rice and cook over a medium heat, stirring, until it has been absorbed. Continue to add the broth in this way, allowing the last ladleful to be absorbed before adding the next and stirring frequently.

5 When the rice is cooked but still slightly hard in the center, carefully stir in the asparagus tips, the remaining butter and the Parmesan cheese. Season to taste with salt and pepper. Serve on warmed plates sprinkled with coarsely grated Parmesan.

POTATO SALAD WITH SMOKED TROUT

Ingredients

1¾ lb / 800 g boiling potatoes

4 tbsp sour cream

2 tbsp mayonnaise

4–5 tbsp vegetable broth (stock)

White wine vinegar, to taste

2 scallions (spring onions), finely chopped

Salt, to taste

1 red onion, sliced

12 oz / 300 g smoked trout, flaked

1 handful fresh herbs, e. g. parsley or cress

2 tbsp capers

Method

Prep and cook time: 50 min

1 Place the potatoes in a steamer basket; set in a saucepan over 1 inch of boiling water. Cover and steam until tender, about 25 minutes. Drain and return to the hot pan to dry briefly, then peel and slice. Allow the potatoes to cool for a few minutes.

2 Mix the sour cream, mayonnaise, broth (stock) and vinegar in a large bowl; add the scallions (spring onions) and season to taste with salt. Add the potatoes and onion and toss gently to coat; spoon onto plates. Scatter the trout, herbs and capers over the salad and serve.

STUFFED TOMATOES

Ingredients

For the tomato sauce:

3 tsp olive oil

1/3 cup / 50 g finely chopped onion

2 cloves garlic, finely chopped

2 sprigs thyme

4 (7-oz / 200 g) beefsteak tomatoes, finely diced

1/2 cup / 100 g tomato concentrate (purée)

1–2 good pinches sugar

Salt and freshly ground white pepper,

For the tomatoes and stuffing:

4 (7-oz / 200 g) beefsteak tomatoes

1 tbsp. butter

1/3 cup / 50 g finely chopped onion

1 bay leaf

1 tsp fresh thyme leaves

1/2 cup / 100 g long-grain rice

1/4 cup / 30 g very thinly sliced carrot

1/3 cup / 30 g thinly sliced celery

1/3 cup / 30 g thinly sliced zucchini (courgette)

1/4 cup / 30 g frozen peas

2 tsp crème fraîche

2/3 cup / 75 g finely grated Gruyère cheese

1 tsp olive oil

Snipped chives, to garnish

Method

Prep and cook time: 1 h 20 min

1 Preheat the oven to 350°F (180°C / Gas Mark 4). Lightly grease a 1-quart / 1-liter baking dish.

2 For the tomato sauce, heat the oil in a skillet; add the onion, garlic and thyme and sauté until soft. Add the diced tomatoes and tomato concentrate (purée) and cook until the tomato is soft. Add 1²/₃ cups / 400 ml water and season with salt and pepper. Cook for a further 5 minutes or so. Check the seasoning and add more salt and the sugar if necessary. Purée the sauce in a blender and set aside.

3 For the tomatoes, cut off about the top third of each tomato to form a lid and set aside. Carefully hollow out the remainder of the tomatoes with a spoon and reserve the flesh.

4 For the stuffing, heat the butter in a skillet; add the onion, bay leaf and thyme and sauté until soft but not browned. Add the rice and sauté for 1 minute, then add ¾ cup / 200 ml water, the carrot and 1 cup / 150 g of the tomato flesh. Season with salt and pepper. Bring to a boil, then reduce the heat and simmer for about 5 minutes, stirring occasionally. Add the celery and zucchini (courgette), then stir in the peas and simmer for about 15 minutes. Stir in the crème fraîche and grated cheese and season to taste.

5 Fill the hollowed-out tomatoes with the rice stuffing and put on the lids. Stand the stuffed tomatoes upright in the baking dish. Drizzle with olive oil and bake for about 20 minutes.

6 Shortly before serving, warm the tomato sauce. To serve, spoon a little of the tomato sauce onto warmed plates, put a stuffed tomato on each and garnish with snipped chives.

SPAGHETTI WITH SHRIMP AND COCONUT SAUCE

Ingredients

14 oz / 400 g spaghetti

1 leek

4 tbsp. oil

1 tsp. freshly grated ginger

2 cloves garlic, finely chopped

1 pinch curry powder

1 cup / 200 g finely chopped pineapple

Scant ½ cup / 100 ml vegetable broth (stock)

Scant ½ cup/ 100 ml coconut milk

12 shrimp (or prawns), deveined and peeled apart from the tail segment

Sea salt

Shredded basil, to garnish

Lemon juice

Method

Prep and cook time: 35 min

1 Cook the spaghetti in boiling, salted water until al dente.

2 Trim the leek and cut into thin strips.

3 Heat 2 tablespoons of the oil and sauté the leek with the garlic and ginger. Stir in the curry powder and pineapple and add the vegetable broth (stock) and coconut milk. Simmer for 1–2 minutes.

4 Meanwhile heat the rest of the oil and fry the shrimp for 1–2 minutes.

5 Drain the spaghetti, add to the sauce and toss to combine. Season with salt, add lemon juice to taste and serve into bowls. Add a few shrimp to each and serve sprinkled with basil.

RICE SALAD WITH LENTILS

Ingredients

1 cup / 200 g wild rice

½ cup / 100 g long-grain rice

1 cup / 200 g brown lentils

3 tbsp olive oil

1 medium eggplant (aubergine), quartered and thinly sliced

1 red bell pepper, coarsely chopped

3 scallions (spring onions), coarsely chopped

Salt and freshly ground pepper, to taste

1 tbsp chopped fresh parsley

For the garlic dressing:

6 tbsp olive oil

Juice of 1 lemon

4 cloves garlic, chopped

1 pinch sugar

Salt and freshly ground pepper, to taste

Method

Prep and cook time: 1 h

1 Cook the wild and long-grain rice and lentils according to the package instructions; drain and keep warm.

2 Heat the oil in a large skillet over medium heat; add the eggplant (aubergine) and fry until golden brown, turning frequently. Add the bell pepper, reduce the heat, cover and cook until soft, adding 2–3 tablespoons water if necessary to prevent sticking. Stir in the scallions (spring onions) towards the end of cooking time. Gently stir in the cooked rices and lentils. Season to taste with salt and pepper. Let cool to room temperature, then stir in the parsley and adjust the seasoning if necessary.

3 To prepare the dressing, in a blender or mini food processor, pulse the oil, ¼ cup of water, lemon juice, garlic, sugar, salt and pepper until smooth.

4 Spoon the rice salad into bowls and serve sprinkled with the garlic dressing.

MINI SAVORY TARTS

Ingredients
Makes 12 mini tarts

1 cup / 200 g sun-dried tomatoes in oil

14 oz / 400 g thawed frozen puff pastry

3 mini mozzarella balls, thinly sliced

1 small eggplant (aubergine), thinly sliced

Salt and freshly ground pepper, to taste

4 tbsp pine nuts, toasted

Olive oil, as needed

1 handful arugula (rocket) leaves, trimmed, to garnish

Method
Prep and cook time: 40 min

1 Preheat the oven to 400°F (200°C / Gas Mark 6). Line a baking sheet with foil or parchment.

2 Finely chop the tomatoes, adding a little of the tomato oil, until they resemble a paste.

3 Roll out the puff pastry and cut out 12 circles using a 3-inch (8 cm) round cookie cutter. Spoon some of the tomato mixture on the top and season with salt and pepper. Top with a few slices of mozzarella, followed by eggplant (aubergine) slices. Sprinkle with a few pine nuts and drizzle lightly with olive oil.

4 Place tarts on the baking sheet and bake until lightly browned, about 15 minutes. Garnish with the arugula (rocket) leaves and serve immediately.

BEAN AND CHEESE QUESADILLAS

Ingredients

1 tbsp vegetable oil

7 oz / 200 g bacon, diced

2 mild green chili peppers, sliced into rings

1 clove garlic, minced

1 tbsp tomato paste

1 (14 oz / 400 g) can red kidney beans, rinsed and drained

Salt, to taste

Cayenne pepper, to taste

4 flour tortillas

Scant 1 cup / 100 g shredded cheddar cheese

Method

Prep and cook time: 25 min

1 Preheat the oven to 400°F (200°C / Gas Mark 6). Line a cookie (baking) sheet with foil or parchment.

2 Heat the oil in a skillet; add the bacon, chilies and garlic and fry until the bacon is cooked through. Stir in the tomato paste and 3–4 tablespoons of water; add the beans and simmer, stirring, 2–3 minutes. Season with salt and cayenne.

3 Spread the bean mixture onto the tortillas, top with cheese and fold in half. Place on the cookie sheet lined with parchment paper and bake until golden brown, about 10 minutes.

EGG NOODLES
WITH CHICKEN
AND VEGETABLES

Ingredients

8 oz / 225 g dried egg noodles

4 tsp. sesame oil

4 oz / 100 g boneless, skinned chicken breasts, cut into fine shreds 2 inches / 5cm long

2½ tbsp vegetable oil

2 tsp light soy sauce

2 tsp dark soy sauce

1 tbsp rice wine or sherry

1 tsp salt

½ tsp freshly milled pepper

½ tsp sugar

3 tbsp finely chopped scallions (spring onions)

1 tbsp finely chopped garlic

2½ cups / 50 g finely shredded snow peas (mangetout)

1/3 cup / 50 g finely shredded cooked ham

For the marinade:

2 tsp light soy sauce

2 tsp rice wine, or dry sherry

1 tsp sesame oil

½ tsp salt & ½ tsp pepper

Method

Prep and cook time: 30 min plus 10 min to marinate

1 Cook the noodles in a large pan of boiling water for 3–5 minutes, then drain and refresh in cold water. Drain thoroughly, toss with 3 teaspoons of the sesame oil and set aside.

2 Combine the shredded chicken with all the marinade ingredients, mix well and marinate for about 10 minutes.

3 Heat a wok over a high heat. Add 1 tablespoon of the vegetable oil and when very hot and slightly smoking add the shredded chicken. Stir-fry for about 2 minutes and then transfer to a plate. Wipe the wok clean. Add the noodles, soy sauces, rice wine or sherry, salt, pepper, sugar and scallions (spring onions). Stir-fry for 2 minutes.

4 Reheat the wok until it is very hot, then add the remaining oil. When the oil is slightly smoking add the garlic and stir-fry for 10 seconds. Then add the snow peas (mangetout) and ham and stir-fry for about 1 minute.

5 Return the chicken and any juices to the noodle mixture. Stir-fry for 3–4 minutes, or until the chicken is cooked. Add the remaining sesame oil and give the mixture a few final stirs. Turn onto a warm platter and serve at once.

PENNE WITH TOMATOES AND GORGONZOLA

Ingredients

4½ cups / 500 g penne

9 oz / 250 g baby plum tomatoes

7 oz / 200 g tub crème fraîche

Salt & freshly milled pepper

7 oz / 200 g Gorgonzola cheese

Basil leaves, to garnish

Method

Prep and cook time: 35 min

1 Preheat the oven to 400°F (200°C / Gas Mark 6). Cook the penne in boiling, salted water until al dente, refresh in cold water and drain.

2 Halve the tomatoes. Mix with the penne and crème fraîche and season with pepper and a little salt.

3 Put into a fireproof dish and crumble the Gorgonzola over the pasta and tomatoes. Put into the preheated for 10–15 minutes. Serve scattered with basil.

SPINACH AND EGG STRUDEL

Ingredients

2 tbsp butter

1 onion, finely chopped

1½ lb / 750 g spinach leaves, about 10 cups

Salt and freshly ground pepper, to taste

Ground nutmeg, to taste

²/3 cup / 150 g crème fraîche

1 egg

1 tbsp finely chopped parsley

1 (11-oz / 300 g) package frozen puff pastry, thawed

4 hard-cooked eggs, shelled and halved lengthwise

Milk, for brushing the pastry

Method

Prep and cook time: 1 h

1 Preheat the oven to 425°F (220°C /Gas Mark 7). Line a baking sheet with parchment or foil.

2 Melt the butter in a large skillet, add the onion and sauté until tender. Add the spinach and cook, stirring, until wilted; continue cooking gently for about 6 minutes. Season with salt, pepper and nutmeg; set aside and let cool.

3 Whisk together the crème fraîche and egg until smooth; add the parsley and stir into the spinach mixture.

4 Roll out the pastry onto a lightly floured surface. Spread the spinach filling on one third of the pastry, arrange the eggs on top, press in lightly and roll up the pastry. Brush with milk. Put the strudel on the baking sheet bake until golden brown, 30–35 minutes.

CREAMY CORN CHOWDER

Ingredients

1 tbsp. olive oil

1 white onion, finely chopped

2 cloves garlic, finely chopped

1 red chili, deseeded and finely chopped

1 tsp. curcuma (turmeric)

2 small sprigs fresh rosemary

2 cans corn, drained weight 10 oz / 300 g

Juice of 1 lime

3 cups / 750 ml vegetable broth (stock)

½ cup / 100 g whipping cream

2 tomatoes, deseeded and diced

Salt & freshly milled pepper

Method

Prep and cook time: 30 min

1 Heat the olive oil in a skillet and sauté the onion, garlic and chili until soft. Add the curcuma (turmeric), a sprig of rosemary, and half of the corn and stir. Now pour in the lime juice, vegetable broth (stock) and cream. Cover with a lid and simmer for about 8 minutes.

2 Purée with a hand blender until smooth, then strain through a sieve into a saucepan. Bring to a boil. Add the remaining corn and the diced tomatoes.

3 Season to taste with salt and pepper. Garnish with a spring of rosemary and serve.

EGG AND TOMATO WRAP

Ingredients

4 eggs, hard boiled

¼ cup / 80 g salad cream or mayonnaise, more if required

1–2 tbsp. mustard, medium strength

1–2 tbsp. white wine vinegar

2–3 tbsp. sour cream

Salt & freshly milled pepper

2 tomatoes, diced

1 red bell pepper, deseeded and diced

1 large boiling (waxy) potato, cooked and diced

2 scallions (spring onions), trimmed and cut into rings

4–6 large wholewheat tortillas

Method

Prep and cook time: 25 min

1 Peel the eggs and cut into cubes. Mash the egg yolks and mix to a smooth paste together with the salad cream (or mayonnaise), mustard, white wine vinegar and sour cream. Season to taste with salt and pepper.

2 Add the tomatoes, bell pepper, potato, egg and scallions (spring onions) to the salad cream dressing and mix well. Spread the tomato and egg salad on top of the tortillas and roll up into a wrap. Cut in half, season with freshly milled pepper and serve in a bowl.

LENTIL SOUP WITH HAM

Ingredients

Generous 1 cup / 200 g brown lentils

2 tbsp oil

1 cup / 200 g bacon or
pancetta, diced

2 carrot, peeled and finely diced

1 onion, finely chopped

1 large potato, peeled and finely diced

2 bay leaves

2 tbsp sour cream

Thyme, to garnish

Method

Prep and cook time: 1 h plus soaking time: 12 h

1 Rinse the lentils and soak overnight. Rinse again and drain.

2 Put the oil into a hot pan and sauté the bacon until the fat begins to run. Add the diced vegetables, cook for about 5 minutes then add about 2 cups / 500 ml of water.

3 Add the drained lentils and bay leaves and simmer over a low heat for about 45 minutes. Stir from time to time and add more water if necessary.

4 Stir in the sour cream, season to taste and serve garnished with thyme.

CHICKEN SALAD PITAS

Ingredients

1 small grilled or roasted chicken

Scant 1 cup / 200 g mayonnaise

Scant ½ cup / 100 g sour cream

½ bunch parsley (about 1 oz / 25 g), chopped (reserve a few whole leaves for garnish)

1 red onion, coarsely chopped

1 tart green apple, cored, cut into eighths, and thinly sliced

1 clove garlic, minced

Salt and freshly ground pepper, to taste

4 pita breads, halved and split to make pockets

4–6 lettuce leaves

Method
Prep and cook time: 20 min

1 Skin the chicken, take the meat off the bone and shred or cut the meat into small pieces.

2 Combine in a bowl with the mayonnaise, sour cream, parsley, onion, apple and garlic; season with salt and pepper. Line the pita pockets with lettuce leaves, then stuff with the salad. Serve at once, garnished with parsley leaves.

HUMMUS AND SPROUT PITAS

Ingredients

1–2 carrots, peeled and grated

1–2 tbsp vinegar

1-1½ cups / 100–150 g sprouted lentils or bean sprouts

6–8 tbsp prepared hummus

2–4 tbsp sour cream

Salt and freshly ground pepper, to taste

4 whole-grain pita breads, halved and split to make pockets

4 cups (10 oz) / 300 g) mixed salad greens

Method
Prep and cook time: 20 min

1 Mix the carrots in a bowl with the vinegar and sprouts.

2 In another bowl, blend the hummus with the sour cream until smooth and season with salt and pepper. Spread the hummus mixture on one side of each pita pocket, then fill with the carrots and sprouts. Season with a little more pepper, if desired. Serve with salad.

MISO SOUP WITH VEGETABLES

Ingredients

2 tbsp miso

1 tbsp vegetable broth granules

1 bunch radishes, trimmed and halved

1 small carrot, peeled and cut into matchsticks

½ tsp. ground ginger

Salt

¼ nori sheet, cut into thin strips

Method

Prep and cook time: 15 min

1 Put the miso into a pan with 3 tablespoons of water and heat until it dissolves. Add 4 cups / 1 liter water and the broth granules.

2 Add the radishes, carrots and ginger to the soup and simmer for about 4 minutes. Season to taste with salt. Divide the nori strips between 4 bowls, ladle the hot soup over them and serve.

SALMON IN PUFF PASTRY WITH YOGURT DIP

Ingredients

14 oz / 400 g cod fillet

2 tbsp dry white wine

2 tbsp lemon juice, divided

Salt and freshly ground pepper, to taste

²/3 cup / 150 ml light (single) cream

Scant ½ cup / 100 g cream cheese

2 tbsp chopped fresh parsley

1 (11-oz / 300 g) package frozen puff pastry, thawed

About 1 lb / 500 g salmon fillet, skinned

1 egg yolk, beaten

2 tbsp sliced almonds

For the dip:

½ cucumber

Generous ¾ cup / 200 g plain yogurt

Scant ½ cup / 100 g sour cream

Lemon slices, to garnish

Parsley, to garnish

Method

Prep and cook time: 1 h plus 15 min chilling time

1 Prepare the cod stuffing: chop the cod fillet into chunks and combine in a bowl with the wine and 1 tablespoon of the lemon juice; season with salt and pepper. Put into the freezer for about 15 minutes.

2 Place the fish mixture, cream, cream cheese and parsley in a food processor or food mill and pulse until smooth. Return to the bowl, cover and chill.

3 Preheat the oven to 350°F (180° C / Gas Mark 4). Line a baking sheet with parchment or foil. Lay the pastry sheets on top of each other and roll out on a floured work surface to about 3 times the size of the salmon fillet. Place on the baking sheet.

4 Spread half of the cod stuffing on the middle third of the pastry. Place the salmon fillet on top, season with salt and pepper and spread with the rest of the stuffing. Brush the edges of the pastry with egg yolk and fold over the salmon. Brush the top with more egg yolk, sprinkle with the sliced almonds and bake until golden and puffy, 35–40 minutes.

5 Meanwhile prepare the yogurt dip: peel the cucumber, halve lengthwise and scrape out the seeds with a small spoon. Grate the flesh and squeeze it dry in a clean kitchen towel.

6 Combine the yogurt and sour cream with the remaining lemon juice and a little salt and pepper; stir in the grated cucumber.

7 To serve, slice the salmon pastry into 4 pieces, garnish with lemon slices and parsley and serve with the yogurt dip.

CHICKEN AND MANGO SALAD

Ingredients

⅓ cup /50 g hazelnuts, finely chopped

½ tsp hot red pepper (chili) flakes

1½ lb (600-700 g) skinless boneless chicken breasts

2 tbsp vegetable oil

1 tbsp lemon juice

2 tbsp white wine vinegar

2 tbsp extra-virgin olive oil

Salt and freshly ground pepper, to taste

1 (5-oz) bag (150 g) spinach leaves

½ cucumber, thinly sliced

1 ripe mango, peeled and thinly sliced

Method

Prep and cook time: 30 min

1 Combine the chopped nuts with the hot pepper flakes and spread on a plate. One at a time, add the chicken breasts and lightly coat on all sides, pressing crumbs firmly to help them adhere.

2 Heat the vegetable oil in a skillet and fry the chicken until browned on all sides and cooked through, about 10 minutes. Transfer chicken to a plate and keep warm. Return the skillet to the heat and add the lemon juice, 2–3 tablespoons of water, vinegar and olive oil; cook, stirring to loosen browned bits from the skillet, until slightly thickened. Season with salt and pepper.

3 Slice the chicken and arrange on plates with spinach, cucumber, and mango. Drizzle with the sauce and serve at once.

ASPARAGUS AND POTATOES

WITH CREAMY HOLLANDAISE SAUCE

Ingredients

1 ¾ lb / 800 g boiling potatoes

2 tbsp lemon juice

½ tsp salt

1 pinch sugar

1 tbsp lemon juice

16 white asparagus, trimmed and peeled

16 green asparagus, trimmed

Hollandaise sauce:

½ tbsp lemon juice

½ tbsp white wine vinegar

2 large egg yolks

1 stick / 4 oz /110 g butter

Salt and freshly ground white pepper

In addition:

Chopped parsley and chives, to garnish

Method

Prep and cook time: 40 min

1 Cook the potatoes in plenty of boiling salted water for about 20 minutes, until soft; drain and set aside. Keep warm.

2 Bring a pan of water to a boil with ½ tsp salt, the sugar and lemon juice. Add the white asparagus and cook for 12–15 minutes (depending on thickness) until tender. Add the green asparagus for the last 3–5 minutes of cooking time (depending on thickness) and cook until tender. Drain well.

3 For the hollandaise sauce: heat the lemon juice and vinegar in a small pan over a low heat.

4 Put the egg yolks into a heatproof bowl over a pan of simmering (not boiling) water and whisk in the vinegar mixture.

5 Heat the butter in a small pan until just melted. Remove from the heat.

6 Pour the butter in a thin, slow, steady trickle into the egg yolks, whisking constantly until smooth and thick. Season to taste with salt and pepper.

7 Put the potatoes into a serving dish and sprinkle with chopped parsley. Place the asparagus on a serving plate and spoon over a little of the sauce. Garnish with chives. Serve with the remaining sauce in a bowl or jug.

FRITTATA WITH SMOKED SALMON AND MASCARPONE

Ingredients

Makes 2 frittatas

2 potatoes, peeled

2 tbsp vegetable oil

2 tbsp butter

1–2 mild red chili peppers, deseeded and finely diced

8–10 eggs

Salt and freshly ground pepper, to taste

12 oz / 300–400 g smoked salmon fillet, sliced into thin strips

3 scallions (spring onions), sliced into 2-inch / 5 cm strips

4–6 tbsp mascarpone

Method

Prep and cook time: 25 min

1 Cook the potatoes in a pan of boiling water. Drain and shred the cooked potatoes.

2 Add a tablespoon each of oil and butter to a medium nonstick skillet. Sauté the shredded potato and chilies for 1–2 minutes. Leave half of the mixture in the skillet and set aside the rest for the second frittata.

3 Beat the eggs with a little salt and pepper in a medium bowl and pour half of the egg mixture over the potatoes in the skillet. Scatter half of the salmon and scallions on top, stir gently, cover and cook over low heat for 8-10 minutes, until the eggs are set. Wrap the frittata in foil to keep it warm while you cook the second one.

4 Season with salt and pepper. Garnish with a few spoonfuls of mascarpone and serve.

Published by Transatlantic Press

First published in 2010

Transatlantic Press
38 Copthorne Road, Croxley Green, Hertfordshire WD3 4AQ

© Transatlantic Press

Images and Recipes by StockFood © The Food Image Agency

Recipes selected by Jonnie Léger, StockFood

ISBN 978-1-908533-60-9

Printed in China